Contents

Extreme fish

Think you know everything about fish? Think again! All fish live in water and have **gills** and **fins**. But the differences between fish are what make them **extreme**.

Extreme body parts help this frogfish to hide.

Bizarre features or behaviour may help fish to find **mates** or food – or avoid getting eaten themselves!

Fish that go fishing

Anglerfish have fishing rods growing from their heads. There are even fake worms at the end! **Prey** swim over to eat the "worms". They find out it's a trap when the fish's jaws go snap!

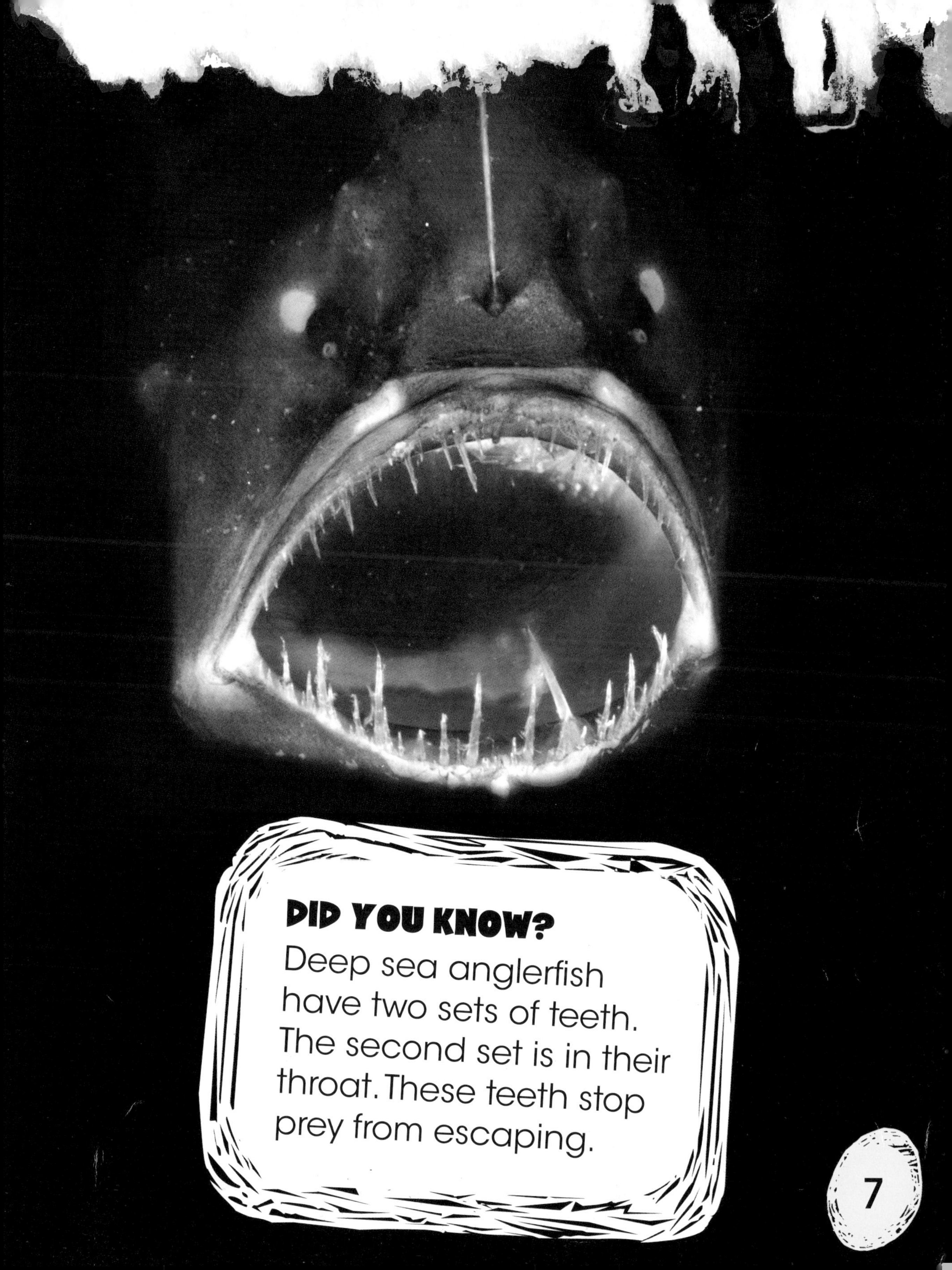

DID YOU KNOW?

Deep sea anglerfish have two sets of teeth. The second set is in their throat. These teeth stop prey from escaping.

Armed archers

Archerfish don't wait for **prey** to come to them. They use their mouths like a water pistol and shoot it down!

If prey is close enough, archerfish leap out of the water to grab it.

Adventurous eels

Eels are fish that like to break rules. Some eels can:

- swim backwards
- change from males into females
- leave the water and wriggle over land
- sneak into gardens to eat vegetables and earthworms.

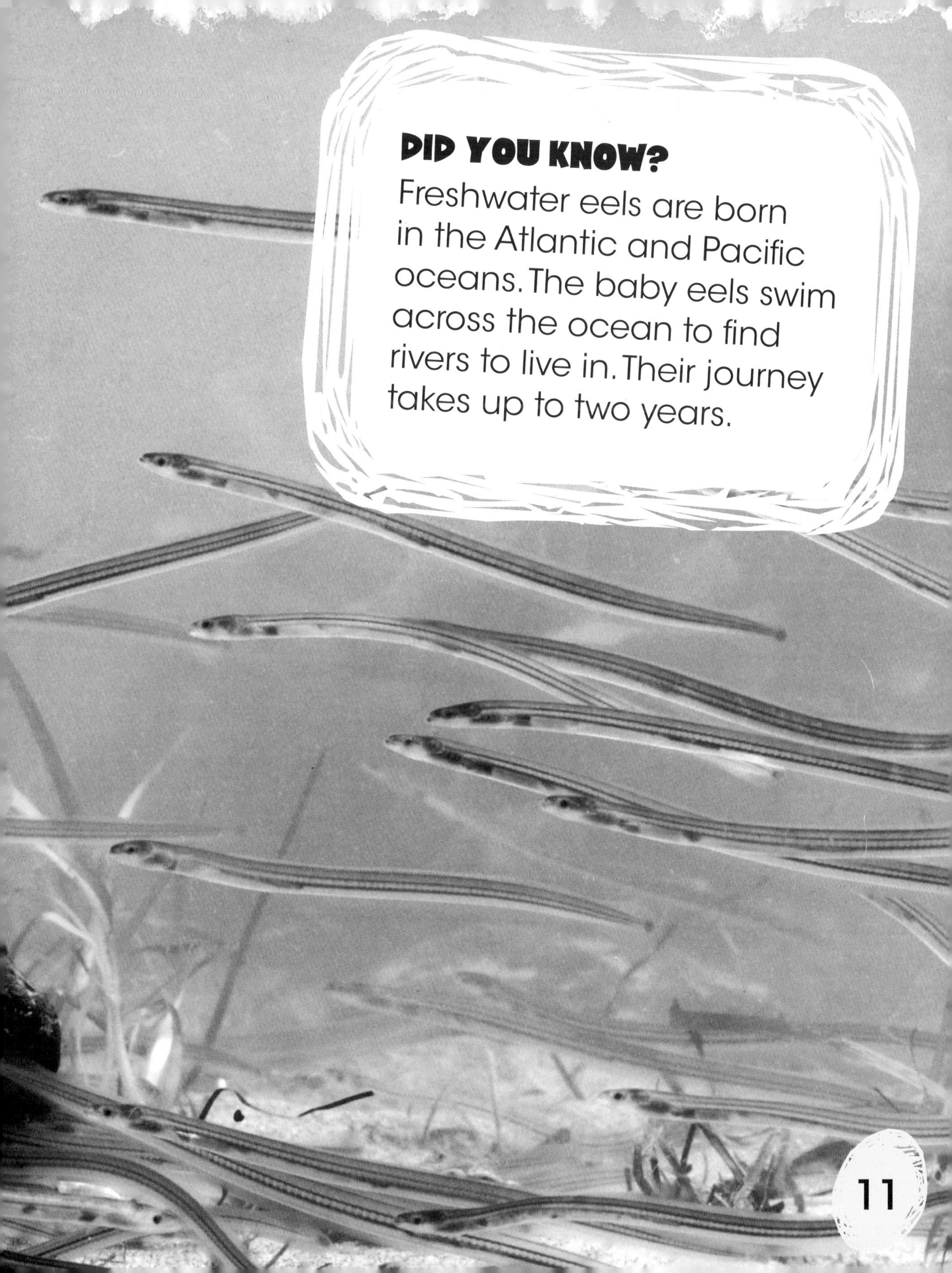

DID YOU KNOW?

Freshwater eels are born in the Atlantic and Pacific oceans. The baby eels swim across the ocean to find rivers to live in. Their journey takes up to two years.

What a shock!

Electric eels have a special skill. They can give **prey** an electric shock! This **paralyses** the prey and makes it easy to eat.

The shock from an electric eel is big enough to knock a horse off its feet!

Shark bites

A shark's teeth are replaced often. This keeps them super sharp. A tiger shark can bite right through the shell of a sea turtle! It eats everything it can find.

DID YOU KNOW?

All of these things have been found in the stomachs of tiger sharks:

- suit of armour
- half a crocodile
- hen house full of chickens
- rubber tyre
- a missing sailor.

How do you hide from a hammerhead shark? Standing in the dark being completely still and silent won't help. The shark will be able to sense your heartbeat!

The hammerhead shark's weird head is very sensitive. It can sense tiny amounts of electricity in the bodies of fish. Even a fish buried under sand cannot hide!
ray buried in sand

Don't step on a stonefish!

Stonefish are one of the most deadly fish in the world. Their **venomous spines** can kill a human. When **prey** swims past, stonefish attack so fast that a normal video camera cannot record it.

The stonefish's amazing **camouflage** makes it look like rock or coral.

Fishy whiskers

A catfish is like a giant, swimming tongue. Its body is covered in taste buds. It has the best sense of taste in the animal world. It uses **barbels** around its mouth to find food. A catfish can taste a meal before it catches it!

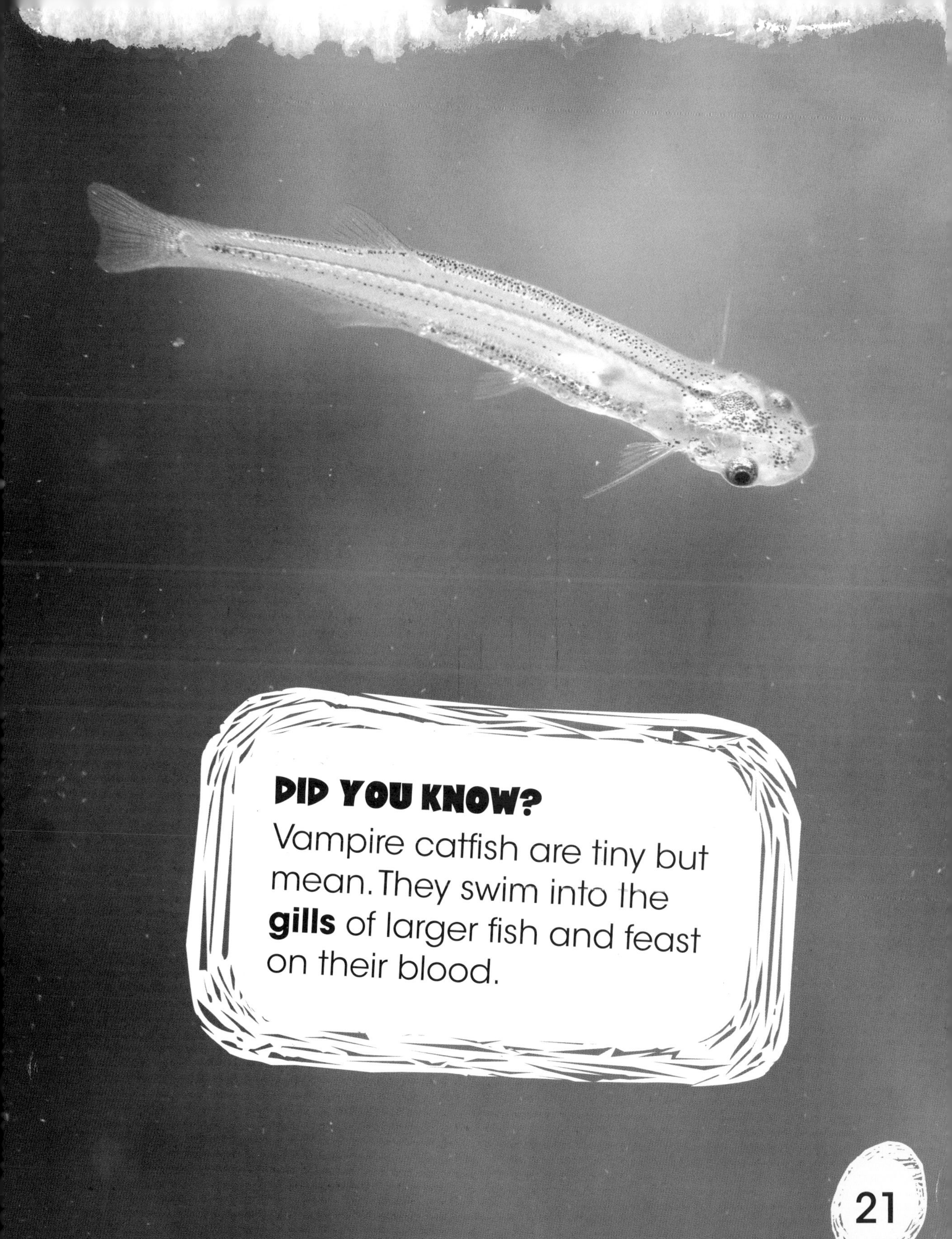

DID YOU KNOW?

Vampire catfish are tiny but mean. They swim into the **gills** of larger fish and feast on their blood.

Prickly porcupine fish

Small fish need to avoid being eaten. Porcupine fish can make themselves impossible to swallow. They puff up their bodies by sucking in water or air. In seconds, they are two or three times bigger. Their long **spines** can stick out up to five centimetres.

Only a tiger shark would dare to swallow this prickly ball!

Fantastic flying fish

Flying fish have an **extreme** way to escape **predators**. They vanish! They do this by leaping out of the water. Their enormous **fins** allow them to glide through the air.

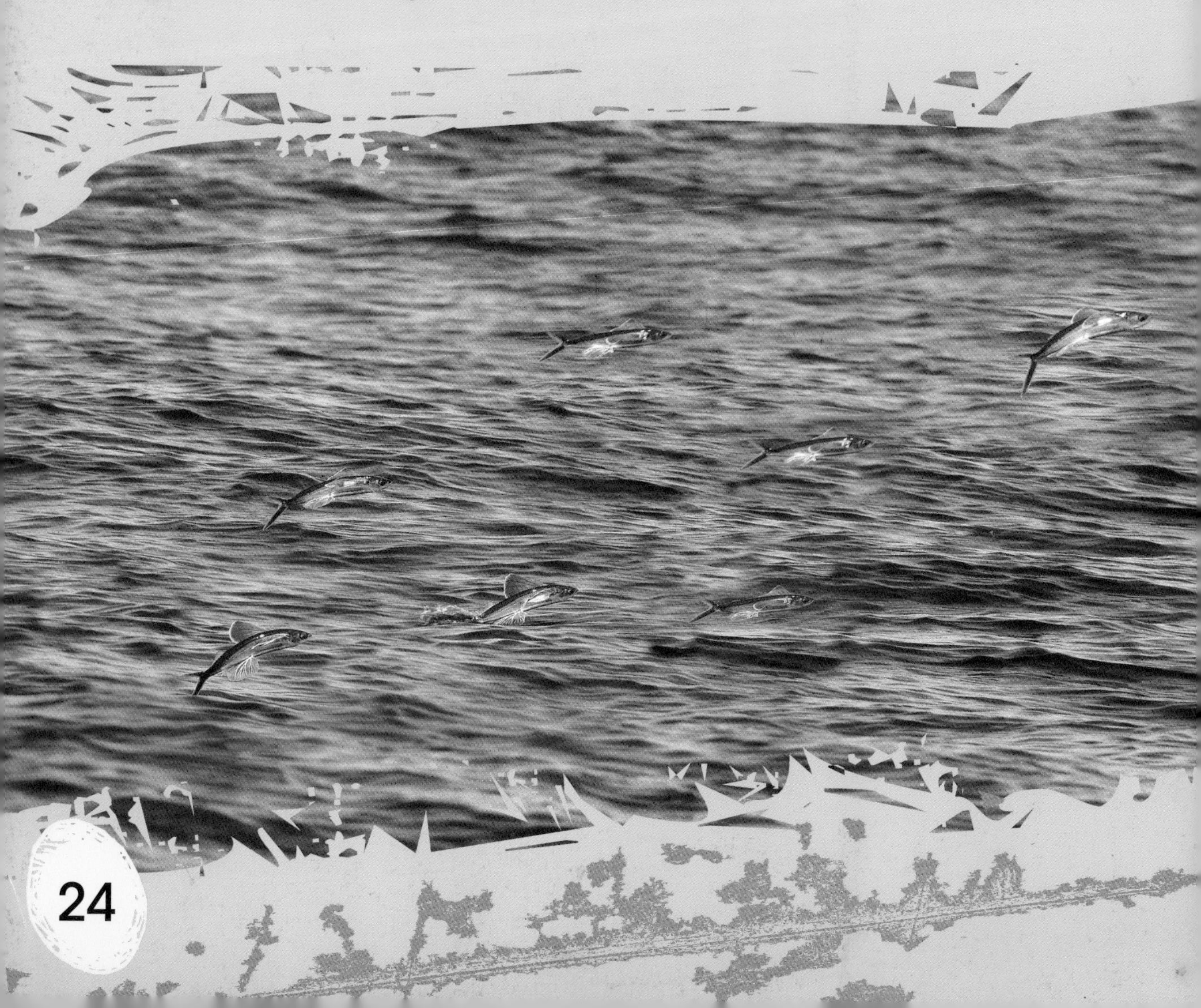

fin
Flying fish beat their tails against the water as they glide. They can stay in the air for 45 seconds.

Unstoppable lungfish

Lack of rain is bad news for most fish. Their **gills** only work under water. But lungfish can breathe air, too. When their river or lake dries up, lungfish bury themselves in a **mucus cocoon**. Lungfish can survive inside the dried mucus for more than four years.

mucus
cocoon

Record-breakers

Which fish do you think is the most **extreme**? Why? Have a look at some of these record-breaking fish to help you decide.

What? Flying fish

Why? Longest journey out of water

Wow! Flying fish can leap up to 10 metres above the water. That's about the height of five doors on top of each other!

What? Piranha

Why? Most people eaten by fish in one sitting

Wow! In 1981 a boat sank in Brazil. Piranhas killed and ate more than 300 passengers.

What? Whale shark

Why? Largest fish

Wow! These monsters of the deep can grow more than 12 metres long – longer than a double decker bus!

What? Frilled shark

Why? World's longest pregnancy

Wow! Each frilled shark pregnancy lasts for up to three-and-a-half years!

What? Death puffer

Why? Most poisonous to eat

Wow! The poisonous skin, blood, and liver of puffer fish can kill a person in just 20 minutes. They are popular meals in Japan – with the poisonous bits removed!

What? Orange roughy

Why? Longest-living

Wow! These slow-growing fish often live to celebrate their 150th birthdays!

barbel whisker-like body part on the heads of certain fish, such as catfish

camouflage colours or markings that help an animal to blend in with the things around it

cocoon case or covering used to protect an animal

extreme unusual, amazing, or different from normal

fin thin, flat body part of a fish, used for swimming

gills body part for breathing, used by fish and other animals that live in water

mates two animals that can have baby animals together

mucus thick, slimy liquid used to protect certain parts of an animal's body

paralyse take away the ability to move

predator animal that hunts other animals for food

prey animal that is hunted by another animal for food

spine sharp, pointed body part that sticks out on some animals

venomous able to give a poisonous bite or sting

Find out more

Books

Shark vs Penguin (Predator vs Prey), Mary Meinking (Raintree, 2012)

Sharks (3D Readers) (Parragon Books, 2012)

Killer Fish (Wild Predators), Andrew Solway (Raintree, 2005)

Websites

Watch flying fish glide:
www.bbc.co.uk/nature/life/Flying_fish#p00f26zt

Check out some amazing facts and photographs of the puffer fish:
kids.nationalgeographic.com/kids/animals/creaturefeature/pufferfish

Index